TAILS from History

A Pony with Her Writer

THE STORY OF **MARGUERITE HENRY** AND **MISTY**

By Thea Feldman
Illustrated by Rachel Sanson

Ready-to-Read

Simon Spotlight
New York London Toronto Sydney New Delhi

SIMON SPOTLIGHT
An imprint of Simon & Schuster Children's Publishing Division
1230 Avenue of the Americas, New York, New York 10020
This Simon Spotlight edition November 2019
Text copyright © 2019 by Simon & Schuster, Inc.
Illustrations copyright © 2019 by Rachel Sanson
All rights reserved, including the right of reproduction in whole or in part in any form.
SIMON SPOTLIGHT, READY-TO-READ, and colophon are registered trademarks of Simon & Schuster, Inc.
For information about special discounts for bulk purchases, please contact Simon & Schuster Special
Sales at 1-866-506-1949 or business@simonandschuster.com.
Manufactured in the United States of America 0919 LAK
10 9 8 7 6 5 4 3 2 1
Library of Congress Cataloging-in-Publication Data
Names: Feldman, Thea, author. | Sanson, Rachel, illustrator.
Title: A pony with her writer / by Thea Feldman ; illustrated by Rachel Sanson.
Description: New York : Simon Spotlight, 2019. | Series: Tails from history | Audience: Age 5–7.
Identifiers: LCCN 2018061203 | ISBN 9781534451544 (hc) | ISBN 9781534451537 (pbk) |
ISBN 9781534451551 (eBook)
Subjects: LCSH: Henry, Marguerite, 1902–1997—Juvenile literature. | Chincoteague pony—Anecdotes—
Juvenile literature. | Misty (Fictitious character : Henry)—Juvenile literature. | CYAC: Chincoteague
Island (Va.)—Juvenile literature.
Classification: LCC SF315.2.C4 F45 2019 | DDC 636.1/6—dc23
LC record available at https://lccn.loc.gov/2018061203

It was July 1946. Something very special was happening on Chincoteague (say: SHING-kuh-teeg) Island in Virginia.

It was an event called
the Pony Penning.
Thousands of people
were gathered along the shore.

Then they started cheering.
In the distance they could see
ponies swimming in the ocean!

Right next to Chincoteague
is an island called Assateague
(say: AAH-suh-teeg).
Many wild ponies live there.

For most of the year
these ponies run free.
They eat grass and
drink a lot of fresh water.

However, during the Pony Penning
the townspeople gather up
some of the wild ponies.
They all walk to the shore.

Then the ponies swim
from Assateague Island
to Chincoteague Island!

Once they reach Chincoteague,
the ponies gallop through the town.

People attend the Pony Penning from all over the world. Marguerite Henry was one of those people in 1946. She wrote books for children and was looking for new story ideas.

While Marguerite was at
the Pony Penning, she heard about
a beautiful pony named Misty.
Marguerite decided to visit
the Beebe family, who owned Misty.

Misty was still a baby pony,
which is called a "foal."
She had many white markings
on her hair.

One marking looked like
the United States turned sideways.
There were many ponies
on Chincoteague Island,
but only one pony looked like this!

Marguerite was dazzled by
Misty's beauty.
She wanted to take Misty home
and write a story about her.

Marguerite offered to write
about the Beebe family
in her story too.
The Beebes thought that was
a great idea!

They agreed that Marguerite
could borrow Misty.
But when Misty was old enough
to have her own foals, she would
need to return home.

Marguerite returned to her farm
in Illinois. That winter she received
a pony from Chincoteague.
But this pony didn't look like Misty.
She looked more like a goat!

Marguerite thought that the Beebes
had sent the wrong pony.
Marguerite was sad but loved
the new pony anyway.

The pony settled in to
her new home. She liked
eating carrots and
munching on oats.

Finally spring arrived.
The pony shed her winter coat . . .
and revealed her white markings!
The pony was Misty after all!

Meanwhile, Marguerite had been busy writing her new book. In 1947 she published *Misty of Chincoteague*. The story was based on everything that Marguerite had seen at the Pony Penning.

The book became very popular.
Many people wanted to meet Misty.
She visited museums,
school assemblies,
and libraries for story hour.

Misty shook hooves with her fans.
She liked having her ears scratched
and her neck stroked.
She liked all the carrot treats too!

One time Misty and Marguerite
were invited to a conference
for librarians.
It was on the seventh floor.
Misty rode her very first elevator!

Back at home Misty had many friends. She lived with a horse called Friday and a cat called Mom-cat. There was also Brighty the donkey, who inspired another one of Marguerite's books.

Every year Marguerite held
a birthday party for Misty.
Many children attended the parties.
They gave presents to Misty.

In 1957, Misty was old enough
to have her own foals.
Marguerite loved living with Misty,
but she needed to keep her promise.
It was time for Misty to go home.

Misty's farewell party was
her biggest party ever. There were
more than three hundred guests.
She even had a cake
with carrots for candles!

Misty returned to Chincoteague
and became a mother
to three beautiful foals.

Marguerite missed Misty, but she knew that the pony belonged in Chincoteague. No matter where they were, Marguerite and Misty would always be connected by the book *Misty of Chincoteague*!

· Facts About Chincoteague Ponies ·

- Most of the wild Chincoteague ponies do not actually live on Chincoteague Island. Instead they live on the nearby Assateague Island.
- The Chincoteague ponies on the island are feral. That means that a long time ago, they used to be domestic and live among humans, but today they are wild.
- The Pony Penning still takes place every year in July.
- During the Pony Penning, some people buy ponies to take home. This way, the wild ponies that stay on Assateague Island have enough food to eat.
- Wild ponies stick together in small groups called "bands."

· Facts About Marguerite Henry ·

- Marguerite Henry was born on April 13, 1902, and died on November 26, 1997.
- When Marguerite was a young girl, she enjoyed visiting her father's printing shop.
- Marguerite also wrote stories about other ponies, including one called *Stormy, Misty's Foal.*
- Marguerite had her first magazine article published when she was eleven years old.
- Marguerite wrote fifty-nine books during her lifetime.